More Words of the Wise Old Paratrooper

by Robin Horsfall.

Edited by Robin Horsfall

www.robinhorsfall.co.uk

© 2018 Robin Horsfall

All rights reserved. No portion of this book may be reproduced in any form without permission from the publisher, except as permitted by U.K. copyright law. For permissions, questions or requests please contact: LSKA18@hotmail.com

Cover by Ernie McGookin.

ISBN: 9781729166093

RE Horsfall Books

Other books by Robin Horsfall

Unleash the Lioness

Fighting Scared

The Words of The Wise Old Paratrooper

Last Words of the Wise Old Paratrooper

***

Co-authored and edited by Robin Horsfall

www.wiseoldparatrooper.co.uk

All available at Amazon.co.uk

The Author

Robin Horsfall was a soldier from the age of fifteen up to the age of thirty-two. He served with the Parachute Regiment, the SAS, The Sultan of Oman's Armed Forces, The Army of Sri Lanka and was a Major in 'Frelimo' The Army of Mozambique. He studied Karate for most of his adult life achieving the rank of 6th Dan Black Belt until in 2011 a neck fracture halted his career. During his recovery he went to Surrey University and studied English literature and Creative Writing and graduated in 2016.

Married since 1981 this father of five and grandfather of ten started posting 'The Sayings of the Wise Old Paratrooper' on Facebook and later decided to collate them along with his short stories and poetry into a collection. This book is the second in the series.

'Those who have the courage to leave the forest will see the stars.'

Dedicated to the few who inspired me:

Sergeant Mick Cotton. 2 Para

Sergeant-Major John Wiseman 22 SAS

Tom Beardsley SKF

Dr Richard Villar 22 SAS

Dr Paul Vlitos. Surrey University

And most of all my wife Heather who continues to nurse me through cancer.

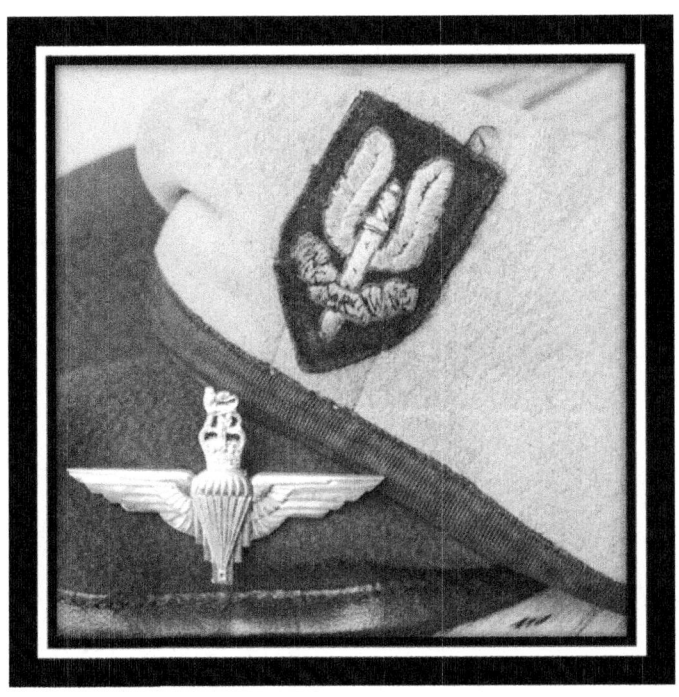

More Words of The Wise Old Paratrooper

Light-weight Para.

Jocky wasn't unusual for a member of 2 Para in the 1970s, he was five feet and four inches tall. Whatever he lacked in stature, he compensated for with tough, aggressive, Scottish pride and high standards.

In 1976 the Battalion was flown to Weiderhausen in West Germany to take part in cross training with the German Falshirmjager Regiment or German paras. We would train together, jump together and after five jumps would gain the right to wear their bronze wings on our battle smocks.

The parachuting took place over two days with the first three jumps from a Transaal C-160D aircraft that we referred to as a 'Small Herc'. We would mount up, fly for ten minutes, jump at one thousand feet, land, drive back and do it again. In the UK it took all day to get one jump organised from a C130 by the RAF. In Germany we could get the whole battalion through three times in one day.

To jump at a thousand or even twelve-hundred feet was a luxury because in the UK we usually jumped at between six-hundred and fifty and eight-hundred feet, which was just enough time to drop equipment, kick out of twists and land. Without any equipment (clean fatigue) we had time to enjoy the jump and shout out to one another. The American T10 'chutes were poor compared to our British P4Xs and several reserves were pulled during the day because of badly developed canopies. The extra height in the sky came in handy when dealing with such incidents.

On day two we finished our quota by jumping from the Bell UH-1

Iroquois helicopter or 'Huey' as it was affectionately known.

Jumping from Hueys was fun, we just sat in the door, waited for the go and pushed off, there was no slipstream to confront and no chance of a collision in the sky. We rotated through as quickly as it took to hit the ground, hand in the used 'chute and put on another.

The weather was warm and still which once again allowed us to enjoy the thrill of flying to the ground without hard landings. The heat gave more lift to the canopy and a lot of guys managed to make stand up landings without rolling to the ground.

The plan was for everyone to complete their remaining two jumps, return to barracks, have a parade, receive our wings and go on the piss. The trucks were standing by to make a quick move back to camp - all in all it was an easy day.

The last lift of the day was ready and Jocky strapped on his 'chute to make his last leap into the void and climbed into the Huey. On the ground fully loaded trucks were already leaving. The afternoon heat hung heavily in the air as the sun started to turn red. The last Huey chugged through the sky and eight chutes appeared against the red evening sunshine. A few moments later seven had hit the ground, everyone looked around for the eighth. A brief search revealed that Jocky was still suspended about eight-hundred feet up waiting to come down. He tried spilling air and steering his chute but to no effect. The swearing of the staff on the ground was matched by Jocky's reply. 'It's noo my fecking fault sir, this bastard thing won't come down.'

It took twenty minutes for gravity to finally take charge and return him to earth. The last chute was handed in and the last truck returned to camp to be greeted by a cheer from the waiting men for the wee, light weight paratrooper whose legs couldn't or wouldn't reach the ground.

***

'Don't talk the talk if you won't walk the walk!'

'Take ownership of your mistakes, they are yours and yours alone.'

'Don't wrap yourself in a national flag and use it as an excuse for stupidity.'

'You can't have a winner without everyone else taking part.'

'Choose your battles carefully and give yourself achievable targets.'

***

Sit!?
I won't sit.
I'm not a dog.
Dogs are like people.
Sniff, touch, follow, agree.
The desire to bond is canine.
I have always been an outsider.
I visit the dogs and stay for a while.
I sit and I watch on my high seat.
Long ago everyone knew I was feline –
Except for me.
I'm a cat.
PRRRRR

***

'A good life starts with being taught the difference between right and wrong.'

'When people call me 'special' they focus on my attributes, while my focus is mostly on my very ordinary weaknesses and faults.'

'When you have reached the top of a mountain sit down for a moment - then look across the valley to the next mountain and set off on your next adventure.'

'If you teach your children to devalue others it is only a matter of time before they devalue their parents.'

***

I.H.A.T.

Lawyers lie
Businessmen buy
Soldiers die.
Kids ask why?
Mothers cry

***

Politics

'Somewhere between the extreme right and the extreme left there has to be the voice of moderation.
Somewhere between hate and murder there has to be the voice of peace.
Somewhere between rich and poor there has to be the voice of decency.'

'Politics is led by fallible people for fallible people. If you want a saint go to church.'

'The law moves in mysterious ways.'

'Just because a policy makes a profit or saves money it doesn't necessarily follow that the policy is morally right.'

'Those who support the execution of political opponents always assume they will be the executioner and not victim.'

'If a nation allows people to behave badly many of them will.' If the police are allowed to behave badly some of them will. If parents allow their children to behave badly most of them will!

'You can kill a man but you can't kill his ideology.'

'Acorns don't worry about splitting the great oaks when they reach for the sky.

'Female soldiers did not win the 'right' to be in the front line. They gave up the 'right' not to be there.'

'When I go over the top don't shoot me in the back for trying.'

'Don't worry about knowing who you are - worry about knowing what you are.'

'When a thinking person with evidence is confronted with belief there is a problem. Belief knows no facts - believers only have faith.'

'If two leaders have reputations as consummate liars then it is impossible to discern the truth. (Trump/Putin).'

'I don't want tough people in charge – I want wise people in charge.'

***

Leadership

'There is nothing impossible to him who will try'

Alexander the Great.

A Greek philosopher said 'Leadership is about setting a good example - for a long period of time.' To understand leadership you first have to lead. No training can prepare you for the responsibility. Being the head of a family is a very good example of leadership. The leader is expected to know all the answers and to make the decisions. Whatever decision is made, it is going to please one party and upset another. Fairness is always demanded, but fairness is difficult to define. Do you share equally or give more to one who needs it most?

The leader does what he or she believes is right and then accepts the disappointment and petulance of the individual that wasn't satisfied. It is the burden he must carry and hope that he or she is right.

In a military society, autocracies, plutocracies or dictatorship, disagreement can be punished severely. This form of leadership is shallow and creates a slow burn of simmering resentment that leads to poor results often with the commanders perceived as the enemy. This system works but it isn't a happy system.

In democratic politics a leader must delegate part of the decision making process to those he trusts and allow them to manage without interference. He encourages, understands and sympathises but he also cajoles and chastises. A leader never makes personal remarks always focusing on the problem and the resolution of the problem. The leader asks his team to bring him solutions not just problems. The leader must make policy. His deputy disseminates tasks to his close and trusted team and he manages their grievances. They are his family. This system gets people to want to do their work. It is a happy system.

Imagine being the Head Teacher in a school with one thousand pupils. The head cannot speak to two thousand parents. The Head must delegate to his or her close and trusted team - his family. Now take a huge step up to Prime Minister and imagine the strength of character required to deal with sixty-eight million people all with their own problems. The PM has six-hundred MPs clamouring for attention and a cabinet that is supposed to be the close and trusted family. A lot of people don't want the responsibility of being parents. Many don't want to worry about how a business is run. Most don't want to lead but a huge number think they know how a leader should lead. It's a huge task and often a thankless one. So when you have a problem with a leader or their policies no matter how upset you are, stick to the issue, the injustice, the poverty and try not to make crude, personal remarks. They are doing a very tough job and it ages them.

***

'Being polite doesn't automatically imply intelligence and being rude doesn't mean one is stupid. However I know which one I would listen to.'

'Don't film it. Put your phone away and stop it from happening!'

'What I hope for from a friend (and my kids) is enough generosity of spirit to know that I have bad days, I make mistakes and I am only human.'

***

Oh Great Queen USA
Wondrous mother of the free
What have you done to decency?
You gave us strength and hope and joy
And raised us from our knees
Where truth and hope and kindness ruled
You suffer at the hands of fools.

***

'Employing your kids sharpens your management skills'

'If you feel sorry for yourself you'll be the only one who does.'

'Don't be a person who knows everything and does nothing.'

'The most important things in life are breathing, eating, drinking, pooing, peeing and sleeping. Take away one and you are in a bad way.'

***

Donald the Fat Duck.

Donald was a fat duck he was fat because he was born rich. His daddy left him a fortune in grain and worms. Donald spent his life sitting in a high nest watching life around the lake go by. Donald had several girlfriends they would come and visit get a few worms and then move on. Donald loved girls but they unfortunately loved the fast thin Drakes that soared around the lake quacking and flapping. Their slim fit bodies were far more interesting than Donald's grain.

Donald could have almost anything he wanted but he wanted to be like the Drakes. Sad and unhappy he went to the Wise Old Owl for advice.

'I want to be a Drake' said Donald, 'I want to be the fastest Drake on the lake.'

The Wise Old Owl knew Donald well and said 'There's nothing wrong with being fat Donald but if it's important to you try eating less and flying more.' Donald replied that he didn't have time for flying he wanted to be the fastest and if the owl couldn't help he would help himself.

Donald knew that he couldn't catch the Drakes but he could slow them down. That night he put on a free party for all the Drakes in the Lake – a lad's night out - free grain and worms with lots of weed.
The next day all the Drakes felt sick. They couldn't walk and they certainly couldn't fly. Although it couldn't be proved it appeared that the food at the party had been poisoned.

Donald flapped his wings and waddled into flight - once airborne he swooped and quacked to attract the attention of the females. They hardly noticed him the more he quacked the more they quaked among themselves. Donald swooped lower and lower trying desperately to attract attention until finally he dropped too low. One wing tip touched the water and he spun into the lake in a great, humiliating splash.

Later that day he returned to the Wise Old Owl and said 'See Owl I am now the fastest duck on the lake. The Wise Old Owl looked at him for a long time and then said. 'No Donald you are just a fat f..'. The Owl paused for a moment, controlled himself and then said. 'You don't improve yourself by slowing other people down Donald. You are still just a slow, fat - duck.'

***

'Three things you should never write in a post. 'Just saying' - 'No offence' and 'Fact!'

'Heroes are very rare people who knowingly choose to put themselves at personal risk for Others.'

'I'm not as intelligent as I look.'

***

The Ghosts of Iwetheyus.

Spirit in physical home.
His body and shape,
Illusions of suffering
Feels, touches and holds.
He is Iwetheyus.
He is spirit

She knows other pains
Of the soul
Outside her me
Distress, hate, love and fear
She knows Iwetheyus.
She is spirit.

Physical nothings of emptiness
Nowhere, not even here
Vacuums of space

Aware, so somewhere
They are all Iwetheyus!
They are spirit

Whence did it come?
Where will it go?
From nowhere to nothing
Back whence it came
It cannot go. It is Iwetheyus.
It is spirit.

I am here!
Stirred in love
Injured by emotions
Joined in joy
I am Iwetheyus!
I am spirit.

Spirits of Iwetheyus.
Ephemeral ghosts.
I – we – they – us is you - us!
Iwetheus!
Our Great and Wonderful Spirit.

***

'Favours from friends are free.'

'Learn to read, then to think and then to make a viable argument.'

'It's Sunday - so just for one day stop bloody moaning!'

***

Loki's Jest

Cruel Loki's jest was Freyja's pain

She cast him out on Folkvangr

Born with bastards curse was lain

No father, brother would he shield.

Smote he against all friendly word

And render all about him blighted

To be alone in world of hurt

All love of gods and men he slighted

Sad Odin launched his Valkyrie

They soared across the thunderous sky

To raise a man whose eyes might see

Skellee, skelleee, skelleeee, skreeeee!

They burned his soul and shaped his bones

Beat his sinews rent his hide

Cast his heart with heated stones

Taught him wing'ed horse to ride

When Thor did call his warriors forth

With hammer raised to strike his foe

To ride across the rainbow bridge

With beating drums their hate to sow

At Thor's right hand proved he the best

Remembered Freyja's hate and pain

Was Loki's son no longer jest

-

And Odin's foes did all lay slain.

***

'When the 'thought police' prevent opinions from being voiced - Truth is the first one to be arrested.'

'Everything is offensive to someone who wants to be offended'.

'Cooperate with authority but never, never, never be blindly obedient. Question everything, - demand answers, - force the authorities to be responsible to you!'

'Sometimes the message is in what's not said.'

***

Caught Short.

In 1975 the Parachute Regiment was ordered to form a march and shoot team from all three battalions to represent the UK in an international competition. The final ten-man team was formed from the best shots who could march ten miles, complete an assault course and then engage automatic targets up to five-hundred metres away. The winning team would be the one that completed the physical tests in the allotted time and used the least amount of ammunition. We were given six months to prepare and access to ranges across the length and breadth of Britain. On one occasion we found ourselves billeted at Oakhampton Camp in the South West of England. The barracks were basic with few facilities not even a bar or a television. When the work was done at the end of the day a vehicle was made available to take us all to Torquay for an evening out. The truck was too big to take to the town centre because of the high cliffs and narrow winding streets down to the sea so it was parked at the top of the hill and we were given a time to return later that night.

The weather was warm and sunny and we were eager to get to the pubs and the girls near the beach but Big Mick had a more urgent need. He was bursting for a piss and loudly informed us of the fact as he skipped over a low wall at the side of the road. We wandered slowly on waiting for him to catch up but impatience and the fine evening created a distance that separated us for what turned out to be the whole night. Back at the 2300 hours rendezvous with the truck he still hadn't been seen and despite waiting for an extra half hour the vehicle grudgingly returned us all to Oakhampton and bed.

At 0600 the next morning the door of the twelve man room was violently kicked in raising us all prematurely to our hangovers. Mick was stood in the doorway – 'You bastards, you left me!' he shouted among other lengthy expletives. It finally transpired that when he had 'Skipped over the wall, he had vaulted himself into a hundred foot drop down a cliff. After falling thirty feet or so he had been saved by falling into a tree and had hung there in pain for hours until finally being rescued in the early hours of the morning. One under the breath comment was that thanks to the tree he was caught short in more than one way that night.

***

When someone is trying to kill you who do you call? First you call a soldier, then you call a priest, then a diplomat to say sorry, then a policeman to arrest the soldier and then of course a lawyer and finally a politician to take the credit.

'Don't build more "affordable" houses build more council houses.'

'Clever people know that they aren't clever enough.'

***

Fairness

A mother had five children and five biscuits. She asked herself what would be the fair way of dividing them so that everyone got the same? Not one biscuit per child because mum wouldn't get anything to eat, everyone forgets mum! Clearly the fair way would be to break one sixth from every biscuit and give those five pieces to mum, that would be fair.

An aircraft was on fire and about to crash. The pilot had two crew members plus himself sadly there were only two parachutes between three people. What was the fair thing to do?

The only fair thing would be for nobody to receive a parachute and as a result everyone would die. In such a case the fair thing to do is not the same as the right thing to do. Clearly, it would be better to save two people and let one die than to have all three die, it's not fair but it is right.

The point is that just because something is fair it isn't necessarily right and just because something is right it doesn't make it fair. Mums, dads, teachers, managers, soldiers and politicians all have to make right decisions that are unfair.

Next time you want to say 'It's not fair' pause and ask yourself 'Is it right?'

***

'Change is created by optimists.'

'The press are like chainsaws - one slip and they will cut you to pieces.'

'A weak army is worse than no army at all.'

'A father is a man who protects and provides for his children from the day they are born until the day he dies.'

'Love the cake not the cook.'

***

Special Category

A group of people sat in a waiting room, on the table was a pie, knife and a label that read 'Eat me'.

After a brief discussion they all decided that they would share out the pie. However, before they could begin a man spoke up and said 'I deserve more because I am a war veteran and a hero'. Predictably the others disagreed and asked him to explain.

'I have been to war and defended you all against our enemies, I have seen and faced death, I have taken many lives for you and I have saved hundreds.' He picked up the knife to cut the pie.

'Stop' said another I deserve the most because I am a farmer. Every day I face the weather to feed the nation. Without me you would all go hungry. I am a true hero. I deserve the most.'

'No' said another 'I deserve the most because I am a doctor, I have seen and faced death every day at the hospital. I have saved thousands of lives. Without me to tend to the wounded and to deliver the babies you wouldn't be here today.' I am a true hero so I will divide the pie.

The last person in the room was small and timid; when he spoke it was quietly but with great confidence. 'I face death every day, I protect tens of millions and without me you would all be dead. No one will ever call me a hero but you all need me more than soldiers and farmers and doctors. I don't usually get any pie so I will be grateful for whatever I receive.'

The soldier put the knife down and said 'Okay, what is it that you do that is so important?' The little man picked up the knife and as he began to divide the pie he said, 'I clean the sewers'.

***

'Problems don't sort themselves out - you have to do it!'

'If you are going to be wrong be wrong in a positive fashion.'

'Advice is often telling someone what they already know but don't want to hear.'

'A rant happens when a thoughtless idea just won't stop talking.'

'If you are hungry don't ask if the bread is fresh.'

***

60th New Year's Eve.

I was born at the start of the space age. In 1957 Russia put the first artificial satellite into orbit. Rationing of food had just ended although WW2 had been over for twelve years. There were still bomb shelters at the top of Aldershot High Street opposite the Queen public house and the paratroopers wore Pegasus on their shoulder patches.

We were bathed in the sink. Nappies were washed in big saucepans on the stove in Dettol disinfectant.

We walked a mile to school and played until a teacher came into the playground to ring a hand held bell. We formed lines to be marched to class. We sat at desks set in lines and were spanked if we misbehaved. The best meals we ate were the school meals, meat, two veg and gravy. We drank free school milk every day in small bottles to ensure we didn't get rickets.

In the 1960s leaflets were posted through our doors telling us what to do in the event of a nuclear attack. An air raid siren sounded every Friday as a test and to remind us that war with Russia was a possibility.

In the evenings we played in the streets or in one another's gardens, the arrival of a motor car was a rare and significant event that would cause great excitement as it signified a person of wealth. A woman driver was a rare sight. We went everywhere by foot, bicycle or on the bus. The last bus ran at 1030pm.

My mother wore a scarf over her hair when she left the house, we all went to Sunday School. Public bars were for men and women drank half pints or Babycham. Record players and radiograms were the latest trends and every kid was forbidden to have a Beatles haircut.

At weekends we went out and only came home for food. Our friend's mothers were all called 'Aunty'. Currency was pounds, shillings and pence. Twelve pence to a shilling, twenty shillings to a pound, twenty-one shillings to a Guinea. We could buy four blackjacks for a half-penny.

We wrote letters by hand to friends that we called pen-pals. As a cub scout I raised money for charity every Easter on Bob a Job Week. Men earned enough money to feed and house a family and most mothers managed the house and the children. Most of us suffered with

Mumps, Measles and Chicken Pox as children. Diphtheria, Whooping cough, Polio and Scarlet Fever still killed children.

We went to Saturday Matinees at the Cinema and gave our allegiance to the ABC or the Odeon. At the end of the show, we all stood for the National Anthem and saluted the Queen before we were allowed to exit. Boys wore shorts until they were eleven or twelve it was better than repairing torn knees and cheaper than turning down the bottoms on a rapidly growing child. I wore my cap to school until I was fourteen. If I didn't wear it, a Prefect would give me fifty lines to hand in the next day. School leaving age had been raised to fifteen. National service ended.

Wedding receptions were held in the parlour. Birthday parties were about cakes sandwiches and games including 'Blind man's bluff' and 'Postman's knock'.

My Grandmother kept a red bucket by her bed to pee in at night. She would sit by the fire and watch horse racing on the TV and tell me to 'Throw another log on the fire'.

My siblings and I shared a single bed that later became a bunk bed. We put our shirts on under the blankets before we got out of bed in the morning.

My most precious possessions were my bike and my fishing rods.

My world was wonderful and exciting and I hope it is just as exciting for children today.

Happy New Year for 2018.

******

'Always expect the unexpected'.

'When a man loses his dignity he loses everything.'

'You can't educate or convince people by screaming abuse at them.'

'In a short time today will be a long, long time ago.'

***

Someone should do something!

'Someone should do something' said the sheep. 'Someone should speak up'. 'BAA, BAA, BAA.'

Eventually bothered by the constant noise one of the sheep resisted. He refused to obey the dog and left the flock. 'No I won't go' he shouted 'This is wrong, we are all just walking around in circles until the shepherd comes and takes us away to be processed. I'm not going!'

'BAA, BAA, BAA' went the sheep 'Now we're for it, we won't be fed today and it's all his fault. BAA, BAA, BAA.'

The shepherd came later that day with three dogs. He rounded up the protester and put him in the truck to be processed.

'I knew he would come to no good' said the sheep 'He meant well but it's best just to keep your head down and say nothing. BAH, BAH, BAH!'

'Someone should do something' said one of the sheep.

***

'The speaker should not be more important than the message.'

'Sometimes I just don't want to know!'

'Losing an enemy is far harder than losing a friend.'

'When someone tries to lead you by the nose bite their hand.'

***

> Kind words bring life, but cruel words crush your spirit. (Proverbs 15:4 GNT)

Words Kill!

Words are not harmless. Words can make us happy, sad, remorseful or fulfilled. When we are children we are taught how to behave through words, we learn that words used as lies can get us out of trouble and we learn that words hurt.

When we use words that hurt people we hide behind the ancient adage and lie 'Sticks and stones may break my bones but names will never hurt me'. This is one of the great lies because words not only hurt they can kill. When words are used to humiliate other human beings they can make the victims feel so inadequate that they take their own lives. However, this is only one way that words can kill.

Words that convey hatred for others as a group can kill millions. Words began the holocaust in Europe in the 1930s. Hitler's words in Mein Kampf and Goebbels's words as propaganda minister. Without the words used to blame Jews, Gypsies, Homosexuals, Jehovah's Witnesses, Disabled peoples and many more groups the holocaust could not have started. It all begins with ideas and ideas are conveyed in words, communications and messages.

In 1992, Slobodan Milosevic used words to create so much fear of others that it led to one hundred thousand murders in Bosnia. A genocide of Muslims by their Orthodox Christian neighbours; all started with words.

Treaties are written as words. Many treaties were made with the Home Nations of the American continent. The Amerindians believed the words that promised them safety and a small piece of their own land. They laid down their arms. What followed was genocide.

Words are a weapon as dangerous as any gun or bomb. Weapons need to be used carefully and responsibly because they are dangerous. We have freedom of speech in our society to prevent oppression but that freedom like any right cannot be unlimited. Unlimited access to weapons is unthinkable but we all have unlimited access to words. When people offend with words, it is 'freedom of speech' but when people oppress with words it is tyranny. Oppression with words is the first step to oppression with guns.

When we use words on social media or as journalists in the national press or even as presenters on television we should all be under an obligation to use our weapons (words) responsibly. Many words that I hear and read today reflect the emotions of previous generations the words that led to so much human suffering.

We must use words to protect and defend others not as a method to cause pain, hatred and death. Next time we write or speak we must think carefully about where our words are pointed and the damage they can do.

***

Language

'Language gives us the power to soothe or to torture.'

'Crude insults will improve your opponent's standing.'

'When we live in the light we search for the shadows, when we live in the shadows we search for the light.'

'The best time of my life is now! I'm still here to annoy everyone.'

'Beware the fury of a patient man.'

'The best thing about marriage is that your wife is always there for you. The worst thing about marriage is your wife is always there.'

'The great thing about large families is everyone wants you and the difficult thing about large families is that everyone wants something from you.

'The worst thing about kids is that you never get a moment's peace. The best thing about kids is that you never get a moment's regret.'

Kneeside

There was a young fellow from Tees

Who claimed to have thirty-two knees

When playing football

He astounded them all

By twisting and turning with ease.

Letter to the boss.

In 1972 as boy soldiers we were taught how to write letters to our Commanding Officer requesting compassionate leave. One of our group sent the following:

Sir I respectfully submit this my request for compassionate leave.

My reasons being;

1. My pet goldfish has died.

2. I want to see it before the cat gets it.

I remain sir your loyal and obedient servant.

Junior Private K. Fuller

Z Coy.

***

'Language is a burden if we have to listen to drivel. It is even worse if we have to read it.'

'Freedom of speech means being allowed to speak then ignored.'

'It's much easier to be on the outside shooting in than on the inside shooting out.'

It isn't that I don't care, I do! It's just that for most of my life I want to enjoy the good bits, I want to laugh a little. Switch off the news, watch a film, chill, have a Kit-Kat!

***

'Having the military is like having oxygen - you only realise how important it is when it's gone.'

'Clever men should speak gently to stupid men with big sticks.'

'If you put pigs in a palace it soon becomes a sty.'

'I have several best friends. I married the first and she gave birth to the others.'

***

There was an old soldier from Harrow

Whose nose was excessively narrow

When he started to sneeze

He puffed and he wheezed

And his final result was marshmallow.

***

'Be good at one discipline, then be kind to one person, then do it again.'

'Too much information makes you anxious. Less is more!'

'It can be difficult to recover from a victory'

'You don't borrow money you buy it!'

'Chocolate talks to me'

***

Airborne therapy

Des left the army and after a prosperous interlude as a bodyguard decided to study hypnotherapy and psychology. He later described to me his new 'Airborne Therapy' for depression.

He told me,

'A guy came into my office and sat down. I asked him what his problem was.

> *I'm depressed –*
>
> *What makes you think you're depressed? –*
>
> *My doctor says I am and he gave me these pills. –*
>
> *Hmm, you're not depressed.-*
>
> *I am! –*
>
> *No you're not, you are just messed up.-*
>
> *What do you mean?-*
>
> *Well- what you must understand is that everyone in messed up. Most people are messed up about this much. -*

Des held his hands about twelve inches apart a bit like a man describing the size of a fish he had caught. He then held his hands a few inches wider and said.

You are just a little bit more messed up than most people so say about this much. Now if you were depressed you would need to be this much messed up. –

He then held his hands as far apart as they would go to make absolutely clear what the difference was between 'A bit messed up' and 'Depressed'.

So throw those pills away you don't need them. -

I do need them I do! I'm morbidly obese and I can't cope! –

No, you are not morbidly obese you are fat. Now grow up, stop whining and piss off!'

***

'Freedom of speech' or 'Freedom of the press' should not mean the freedom to destroy people's reputations and livelihoods.

Freedom of speech is not the same as allowing an abuse of power. The bullying and uncaring manner of much of the media is focused on profit not truth. 'Freedom to speak the truth' would be a more useful mantra.

'Don't blame everyone else. Blame yourself for sitting on your hands and doing nothing.'

***

Perfect Shite!

We didn't go to war for you
We didn't sacrifice
We didn't serve our kings or queens
We simply threw the dice.

A job of work and time for thrills
Were all we wanted back
Then in return we'd make the kills
And carry haversacks

We climbed across the mountains
We struggled through the swamps
And wandered over deserts
On marches known as 'yomps'

We didn't die for anyone
Except perhaps our mates
We went and did a job of war
And came home in draped crates!

So when you write your nonsense
With 'served' and 'sacrificed'
When you say we 'Gave our lives'
You're talking perfect shite!

***

'Language is capable of many things, it can complement or offend, it can be beautiful, ugly or just plain vulgar. If language is vulgar then it usually has the intention to offend or to place the speaker in a social category. If I choose not to be in that category it is because I have different standards.'

***

Opinions

'Voicing opinions about politicians is a very important part of democracy. The freedom to comment, insult and disagree are all important aspects of freedom as we know it. While we might disagree with another person's point of view we should not take that disagreement as an excuse for vulgar and personal attacks on those voters and citizens we disagree with. Satire is a very effective way of bringing democratically elected leaders down to earth. In a society which is not free, protestors and satirists are arrested or killed. If you have an opinion then voice it in a manner that will not portray you as violent, unthinking and foolish - or make it funny - that works too. Hate can gather a great following very quickly as it is an emotional response to fear. Fear of losing something, fear of others, fear of the unknown. We are lucky we can speak without being frightened of arrest. Use that freedom wisely.'

***

Old Sweat's sayings

'If you snooze you lose'.

'Expert means Ex - A has been. Spurt - A drip under pressure.'

'I've spent more time in the slipstream than you've spent in the NAAFI queue!'

'Daddies are not indestructible but I am'

'Nobody likes a smart arse but everyone needs one.'

'When going on patrol, first shoot the embedded journalist.'

'We are all expendable'

'Don't stare at me – I know I'm beautiful!'

'Don't call me 'Sir' I'm not a fucking officer!'

'If it's dead eat it. If it's not dead kill it!'

'Don't do what I do. Do what I tell you!'

'It can wait'

***

3 Para

Although Para's have always had a reputation for pushing the boundaries and accepted norms of behaviour 3 Para always managed to push them even further. One evening in 1975 while stationed in Aldershot members of the Battalion wearing steel helmets, webbing and combats took their entrenching tools into town. They arrived and regrouped on a large grassy roundabout that was positioned at the bottom of Aldershot High Street between the Roundabout (formerly NAAFI) Club and the Royal Exchange.

'Okay' shouted one of the corporals 'dig in' and the men began to spit lock the turf (roll it back) and then to dig trenches to create an all-round defensive position in depth. In the centre of the position stood a forty-foot flag pole that was flying the Union Flag. 'Defend the flag' was the call and the men prepared to defend it with their last breath. While the work took place several rounds of ammunition (beer) were delivered to the fighting position and reinforcements arrived in the guise of a few WRACs who tucked themselves tightly in between our brave men with a half of lager with blackcurrant.

As night fell an enemy reconnaissance team discovered their whereabouts during a drive past of the position and informed the local Military Police (MPs). Destruction of private property seemed to be the problem as huge mounds of earth had appeared on the rim of the roundabout with a row of empty pint pots on the top. Pick Helms and spades were positioned threateningly over the parapets in preparation for any assault.

The MPs arrived and immediately cut the resupply lines from the Royal Exchange and it also began to rain. They attempted to negotiate with the commander but he was having none of it. Brave defenders rose up and stood shoulder to shoulder, weapons raised refusing to speak to 'Craphats'. The MPs wisely performed a tactical withdrawal and a civilian officer was sent forward to negotiate under a white flag. As the ammunition (beer) ran out and the mud crept into the girl's shoes the reinforcements retired gingerly to the pub or back to the WRAC barracks at the top of Gun Hill for rest and recuperation (R&R).

Eventually terms were negotiated - the men would be allowed to withdraw with honours and weapons provided they made the fighting position good. Trenches were filled in and turf was laid back to give the roundabout now known affectionately as 'Rourke's Drift' a semblance of its former glory.

The men marched into town banners flying but the Police still had one final task to complete - it was going to be a long night. One determined paratrooper was still at the top of the flag-pole and refused to surrender.

***

'Use your life - no matter how short improving yourself. Train yourself to overcome problems. Develop a generosity of spirit. Stand up to tyranny. Persuade and educate the foolish. Avoid dragging others down it can't improve you. Worry about what you do not what others do. Be firm in your principles but kind in your actions and never let the bastards get you down!'

***

Leeds Seeds.

There was a young fellow from Leeds.

Who planted unusual seeds.

They grew to a height.

That blocked out the light

'Eee bah gum' said the lad, they're all weeds!

***

And now, an intellectual moment.

If I write down numbers sequentially and never stop I can continue for all time but I will only write each number once. I could suggest that if a number can exist only once in infinity then it is also possible that life might only been created once in an infinite universe.

All life on Earth has a single origin, which suggests that life was only created once on one planet in one solar system. This planet was a perfect distance from its star and had a partner planet that kept it stable as it rotated. It had copious quantities of liquid water and a temperate climate.

Such conditions might exist on other planets, statistically it is almost certain - but life? What if earth is the only place where life has formed and we are alone in the whole universe?

We might get to other worlds and discover that there was never life anywhere else. Then we will have to ask the questions– the ultimate questions for all humankind.

Was Gene Roddenberry wrong? Was Stephen Hawking winding us up? Is Pluto a planet? Is Donald Trump an illegal alien? What do women really want?

***

'All IRA terrorists are Catholics.

All Catholics are not IRA terrorists.

All white supremacists are white people.

All white people are not white supremacists.

All ISIS extremists are Muslims.

All Muslims are not ISIS extremists

***

'You can't make an omelette by talking to the eggs.'

'You must learn to be a friend to make a friend.'

'Don't be a spectator when you can be a player.'

'How you feel might be someone else's fault. What you do about it is entirely your own fault.'

'Saying 'FACT!' does not substantiate a statement.'

'You have to learn to cheat - it is instinctive to be fair.'

'Spirit is the flower that blooms from dignity.'

'Think hard before you repeat other people's thoughtless remarks.'

'Listen to the storm before you put the wind in your sails.'

A Gift from my Son

My old man is a hero,

He's brave , he's bold, he's tough

He's protected the famous

The rich and poor

Taught karate and what's more

Created a company that helps

Children thrive,

To stand up to bullies

To make friends with enemies

To respect their parents

To fill them with assurance

Fitness and endurance.

My old man is a hero,

He's brave, he's bold, he's tough.

An English degree at 60

And a political career to come.

There's no obstacle of life

He won't crush or overcome

He wrote a book to help people,

And continues to write much more,

It's a thing I can advise him on

And a gift I thank him for.

The world sees a hero

But I just see my dad.

A man who's an example

But not so cool when he's mad ;)

A proud father and grandparent

Who still has a long way to go

A heart so big and a mind so broad

A wit so quick it can't be stored

More fights to fight

More hearts to ignite

But more loved than he can know.

Oliver Horsfall 2018

Black, Cherna, Negro, Noir, Swartz.

In 2015 I was attending a lesson in English Literature at the University of Surrey. The subject under discussion was Othello. For those who are not familiar with Shakespeare Othello was a Moor, a North African.

At some time during the discussion Othello's ethnicity came under discussion and I referred to Sub Saharan Africans as 'Negroes'. When the class ended I was taken aside by the tutor, a Reader of English Literature who gently warned me that the term Negro was not to be used by students at the University as it might be considered racist or derogatory to black students.

I asked what term she would consider appropriate and she replied that the term 'black' was acceptable. I countered by explaining that the term 'black' is not specific to those whose ethnic base comes from Sub Saharan Africa. I also explained that the word Negro is simply the same word as black in Spanish or Portuguese.

'Black' is simply a sound that communicates a colour. As an adjective that describes people it conveys the colour of skin but incorporates brown as well. Most African-Americans could not claim to have black skin but in truth are brown. I am not white I am better described as light brown. Anthropologists usually refer to humans who historically come from Sub-Saharan Africa as Negroes.

An adjective without context carries no meaning other than to create a description. Green, Blue, Yellow are simply colours. Once a context has been created then the word carries some form of meaning. 'I love the blue sea'. However, there is still no nuance, no intonation and no body language that conveys the true intent of the speaker.

My old Parachute Regiment friends will still insult me as a greeting, I take no offence because I know from the complicated mixture of all of their actions that they are welcoming me in a friendly way. I also know that someone might speak to me in generous terms but their tone is sarcastic or their body language does not fit the words. Words are just sounds until they are incorporated into language with a meaning. The meaning is more than the sum of the words it is the intent of the words. If I intend to offend then my words are offensive - if on the other hand there is no intent to offend either from ignorance or misunderstanding then there is no wrong.

Keyboard Commandos

When you write 'people', 'these people', 'we' and 'a considerable number' please specify who the 'people' are who 'we' are, and what a 'considerable number' actually is.. I will then be better informed as to the true measure of the threat to the nation. Once we have established the size of your threat perhaps then you could provide us with your solution.

***

Pantoum of Old Love

I remember young love
Built on strong foundations
I now know old love
Experience of life's creations

Built on strong foundations
Silence, sharing and peace
Experience of life's creations
Our gradual release

Silence sharing and peace
A joy of sharing
Our gradual caring release
Our long term pairing

A joy of sharing
The time of blending

Our long term pairing
And constant mending

The time of blending
Becoming as one
And constant mending
Never, ever undone.

Becoming as one
Our wonderful path
Never ever undone
Two on one path.

Our wonderful path
I remember young love
Two on one path
I now know old love.

***

Lunch Anyone?

In 1983 B Squadron 22 SAS spent several months training in the jungles of Brunei. The troops worked out from a permanent base in the middle of the Ulu-Tutong. Our maps were in many places white sheets with grid squares marked over nothing – unmapped territory. Out there in terra incognito lived the Iban the native aboriginal tribes of the island. In the past they had been head-hunters and cannibals but the incursions of white men after WW2 had gradually taken them away from their old ways - or so it was said.

The SAS had an old relationship with the Iban from the Borneo conflict in the 1960s. Working behind enemy lines as reconnaissance troops they had obtained the confidence of the tribes by winning 'hearts and minds' mostly by providing medical care.

Remote tribes have long memories and it was hoped that we would encounter them again.

It fell to 6 troop to have just such an encounter. They were greeted joyfully by the head-man of the village and asked if they wished to eat and stay overnight. The hospitality was gratefully accepted on the proviso that they slept in hammocks outside the longhouse. A fire usually burned all day in an Iban village because lighting fires could be time consuming in the wet tropical climate. A stew was prepared in a large pot or cauldron big enough to feed twenty or thirty people on a good day. The very best meats were always prepared on special occasions and on this one it was assumed that a piglet would be sacrificed to the pot.

The day passed well and the medics treated infections and wounds where possible. One trooper noticed a small hairy object about the size of a tennis ball hanging from the waist of a small man with a huge machete and asked what the item was. It turned out to be a shrunken human head. There was no way of knowing or asking how long he had possessed the head but it was clear that some of the *old ways* were still being practised. The man grinned with pride as he showed off his trophy.

Before nightfall everyone sat or crouched just outside the longhouse for the communal meal. The troopers offered their mess tins for a portion of stew. They added and shared a few items from their own rations to flavour the dish such as salt and pepper. Then they humbly tucked in until the cook scooped out what appeared to be a baby's arm and dropped it into the next mess tin with the hand hanging over the side (finger-nails still in place). There was a pause as each man looked at the other and then at the Iban cook and his proud smile. He had clearly saved that bit for a special person. Wary of creating offense but keen to know exactly what was in the stew a question was asked by the local guide attached to the troop as to the contents of the dish. The meal stopped as everyone waited for the translation.

It turned out that the special meat of the day was monkey.

***

'Knowing words is not the same as using them.'

'A man who marries his mistress creates a vacancy.'

'A politely presented opinion does not deserve an abusive reply no matter how much one disagrees.'

'Nationality is not defined by religion.'

***

The Mad Race.

I have grandchildren with brown eyes and blue eyes, – white skin and back skin. Which 'race' do they belong to?

DNA evidence proves that all humans descend from a common ancestor. If there is a race then we are one race, the human race, one people, one tribe. Like the birds we have a wonderful range of shapes, colours, sizes and cultures. The differences make us interesting they don't make us enemies.

'There is no such thing as 'race'! It is a ridiculous concept invented by families or tribes who want to feel superior to others.

C

'When you are very ill you have to worry about how everyone else copes with your illness.'

'Imagine your worst hangover, combine it with seasickness, extend it for seven days and then imagine someone squeezing your heart. That's chemotherapy!'

The three Cs of hell - cancer, chemotherapy and constipation.

***

Suffering.

Oh great spirit how hast thou drained my soul?

My mind fills with all hopes and desires

Yet frailty and weakness overcome my role

And illness wets and drowns my fires

Can I muster - fight and hold good stead?

Or trust to thee and take my rest?

Will weakness reign from either thread?

Is loving thee where knowing's best?

Will daylight dawn and bring me forth?

My mind in turmoil goes awry

To seek for life and love with mirth

Father help me - answer me I cry.

Or shall I just curl up and die

And face alone whatever's nigh?

'They were my mates.'

In 1982 the 2nd Battalion Parachute Regiment began to reorganise as the battle for Goose Green came to a close. A dreadful three-day battle had finally resulted in 650 paratroopers with support arms defeating 1300 Argentinians but with heavy losses.

Dead men had been left where they dropped and now it was time to recover their bodies. No one was completely sure how many needed to be recovered and carrying them on stretchers over long distances wasn't practical. A tractor with a trailer was acquired from a crofter and a small group of exhausted men set out to collect their fallen comrades.

It is touching to see how gentle survivors are when they touch their dead buddies. Only hours before fear and aggression had combined to produce creatures who could kill without hesitation and laugh at crude battlefield jokes. Now they were tender and quiet.

They placed the bodies in zip up bags then laid them side by side on the trailer in as orderly and dignified a manner as they could. Hour after hour they combed the battlefield until finally the light faded and they walked back alongside the trailer to the headquarters.

When they arrived one of the collection team was missing and a search failed to find him. Was he injured? Had they left him behind in the minefields? Eventually he was discovered asleep on top of the bodies. In the dim light he was just another camouflaged body in the pile.

They pulled him off and asked him what he thought he was doing.

'Well' he said 'they were my mates and I wanted to be close to them.'

'It doesn't matter how wise you get - sometimes you just have to kick ass!'

'If at first you don't succeed don't go parachuting'

'Selling weapon's for 'defence' is like selling sex to control VD.'

***

'The big dog doesn't listen when the little puppies bark.'

'Time never runs out.'

'Right and wrong are not dictated by victory and defeat.'

***

'Fining people with no money is like starving people for being hungry.'

'A man dying of thirst dreams of water. A man dying of loneliness dreams of friends.'

'Sometimes we should all stop talking and give our brains a chance to catch up.'

***

'Before deriding the achievements of others contemplate your own achievements.'

'Bad things happen to good people.'

'Plan for all eventualities and you will never get past the plan.'

'Learn from the past but look to the future'

***

Wise Old Paratrooper says

'It's Saturday, stop whining, go down the pub,

watch TV, smile, take the day off and

NLTBGYD!'

www.wiseoldparatrooper.co.uk